"Thy words were found, and I did eat them;
and thy word was unto me
the joy and rejoicing of mine heart:
for I am called by thy name,
O Lord God of hosts."
Jeremiah 15:16

The Bible is the best
Health Book,
Mathematics Book,
Music Book,
Nature Book,
History Book,
Geography Book,
Language Book,
and
Spelling Book!

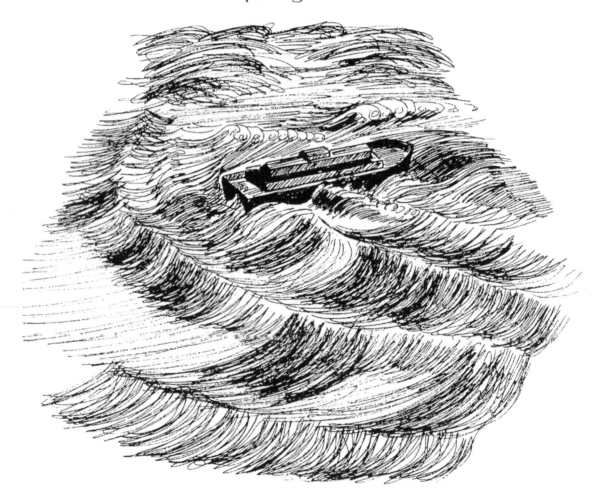

Table of Contents

Table of Contents

Introduction
The Everlasting Covenant

The Everlasting Covenant

"Now the God of peace,
that brought again from the dead our Lord Jesus,
that great shepherd of the sheep,
through the blood of the everlasting covenant."
Hebrews 13:20

The everlasting covenant is the theme for this spelling booklet. Therefore, we will study lessons about the Flood.

"As we look upon this bow, the seal and sign of God's promise to man, that the tempest of His wrath should no more desolate our world by the waters of a flood, we contemplate that other than finite eyes are looking upon this glorious sight. Angels rejoice as they gaze upon this precious token of God's love to man. The world's Redeemer looks upon it; for it was through His instrumentality that this bow was made to appear in the heavens, as a token or covenant of promise to man. God Himself looks upon the bow in the clouds, and remembers His everlasting covenant between Himself and man.

"After the fearful exhibition of God's avenging power, in the destruction of the Old World by a flood, had passed, He knew that those who had been saved from the general ruin would have their fears awakened whenever the clouds should gather, the thunders roll, and the lightnings flash; and that the sound of the tempest and the pouring out of the waters from the heavens would strike terror to their hearts, for fear that another flood was coming upon them. But behold the love of God in the promise: *'This is the token of the covenant which I make between me and you and every living creature that is with you, for perpetual generations: I do set my bow in the cloud, and it shall be for a token of a covenant between me and the earth. And it shall come to pass, when I bring a cloud over the earth, that the bow shall be seen in the cloud: And I will remember my covenant, which is between me and you and every living creature of all flesh; and the waters shall no more become a flood to destroy all flesh'* (Genesis 9:12-15).

"The family of Noah looked with admiration and reverential awe mingled with joy upon this sign of God's mercy, which spanned the heavens. The bow represents Christ's love which encircles the earth, and reaches unto the highest heavens, connecting men with God, and linking earth with heaven.

"As we gaze upon the beautiful sight, we may be joyful in God, assured that He Himself is looking upon this token of His covenant, and that as He looks upon it He remembers the children of earth, to whom it was given. Their afflictions, perils, and trials are not hidden from Him. We may rejoice in hope, for the bow of God's covenant is over us. He never will forget the children of His care. How difficult for the mind of finite man to take in the peculiar love and tenderness of God, and His matchless condescension when He said, 'I will look upon the bow in the cloud, and remember thee.'"*

*7 Bible Commentary 1091

The Covenant
Outline
of the Bible Lessons

I. Noah, His Family, and Character

II. The Ark and Its Cargo

III. The Flood

IV. The Drying of the Waters

V. The Bow of Promise

Instructions

1. This is a teacher's resource, however, much of the booklet may be used with the student.

2. Study the Bible lessons before doing the academic part each day.

3. Each question in the Bible lesson may be answered in the exact words of the Bible, and if so answered, will prove a blessing to the one answering. No human paraphrase can ever equal in power and effectiveness the simple word of God.

4. A memory verse is given with each lesson. More may be added.

5. In the Bible lessons there are words that need to be understood. These are given for special study.

See the section under spelling cards on pages 61-62.

6. Spelling lists may be made from each lesson. See pages 57-58.

7. All these suggestions, and many more, may be given and faithfully followed, and still the Word of God find no place in the hearts of the children. The Holy Spirit's power is needed to change the life.

"How shall I teach Thy sacred Word
To children dear, Oh Lord?
How train young soldiers of the cross
To wield the Spirit's sword?"

This can only be done by much prayer, study, and meditation being used by God and being His instrument.

Lesson I
Noah's Family and Character

Study Genesis 6:1-13.

Readings: Matthew 7:13-14; 24:37-39; Deuteronomy 7:2-4; I Peter 3:19-20; Psalm 14:2-3

Spelling Words: grace, repent, grieved, violence, continually, strive, renown, corrupt, multiply, imagination

Memory Verse: *"As it was in the days of Noe, so shall it be also in the days of the Son of man"* (Luke 17:26).

Review:
1. Whom did the sons of God take for their wives?

2. How long did God say men should live?

3. What special class of persons is mentioned?

4. Who were the mighty men of renown?

5. What was every imagination of men's hearts?

6. How was the Lord affected by their ways?

7. What did He say He would do?

8. Who alone was found doing right?

9. What was the character of Noah?

10. Name his sons.

11. What was the condition of the earth?

12. Who had filled the earth with violence?

Notes: (1) The *"sons of God"* were the descendants of Seth, while the *"daughters of men"* were the wicked children of Cain. For a long time they remained separate, but after a while they began to associate. It is dangerous to associate with wicked persons, except to do them good. When the children of God became closely associated with the children of Satan, they all became wicked (II Corinthians 6:14-16).

(2) The long-suffering of God waited in the days of Noah one hundred and twenty years for men to repent. God is waiting now, in these last days, because He is *"not willing that any should perish,"* but desires that *"all should come to repentance"* (II Peter 3:9).

Lesson II
The Ark and Its Cargo

Study Genesis 6:14-22; 7:1-10.

Readings: II Peter 3:3-12; Psalm 33:18-19; II Timothy 3:1-7; Matthew 24:38-39; *Patriarchs and Prophets,* Chapter 7

Spelling Words: ark, clean, beast, cubit, covenant, food, fowl, cargo, fashion, establish, pitch, house, gopher, righteous, substance

Memory Verse: *"By faith Noah, being warned of God of things not seen as yet, moved with fear, prepared an ark to the saving of his house"* (Hebrews 11:7).

Review:
1. What did the Lord tell Noah to prepare?

2. Of what material was the ark to be built?

3. Give its dimensions in cubits and in feet.

4. How many openings had the ark?

5. Make a list of all that was to be in the ark.

6. How faithfully did Noah obey the Lord's directions?

7. What invitation did the Lord give to Noah and his house?

8. Why were Noah and his household saved?

9. How many clean beasts did the Lord tell Noah to bring? unclean beasts? fowls?

10. For what purpose were all these taken into the ark?

11. How long after all were inside before the Flood began?

12. How old was Noah when he went into the ark?

Notes: (1) Noah showed his faith by his works (James 2:18). He preached not only in words, but also in deeds (II Peter 2:5).

(2) How scornful must the world have been of one who expended all his time, strength, and money in building a boat on dry land!

(3) Leviticus 11 gives the difference between clean and unclean beasts.

(4) All of Noah's family were saved—a reward of his faithfulness.

(5) The cubit is generally regarded as about 21 inches.

(6) "God gave Noah the exact dimensions of the ark, and explicit directions in regard to its construction in every particular. Human wisdom could not have devised a structure of so great strength and durability. God was the designer, and Noah was the master-builder. It was constructed like the hull of a ship, that it might float upon the water, but in some respects it more nearly resembled a house. It was three stories high, with but one door, which was in the side. The light was admitted at the top, and the different apartments were so arranged that all were lighted." *Patriarchs and Prophets* 92-93

Lesson III
The Flood
(2348 B.C.)

Study Genesis 7:11-24.

Readings: II Peter 3:7-13; Matthew 24:38-39; I Thessalonians 5:2-3; *Patriarchs and Prophets*, Chapter 7

Spelling Words: deep, flesh, heaven, nostril, increased, sort, forty, fountain, window, prevailed

Memory Verse: *"The world that then was, being overflowed with water, perished"* (II Peter 3:6).

Review:

1. When did the waters begin to fall?

2. From what two sources did the waters of the Flood come?

3. How long did it rain?

4. Describe the increase of the waters.

5. How high above the mountains did the waters extend?

6. What was the result to every living thing?

7. Who only remained alive?

8. How long did the waters prevail upon the earth?

9. What destruction is coming upon the earth in the last day? II Peter 3:5-7, 10

10. From what source will the elements of the last destruction come? Revelation 20:9; Ezekiel 28:18; Psalm 11:6

Notes: (1) The Flood was the third and greatest curse.

(2) Man misused the blessings of God, appropriating them to his own pleasure and gratification. So it became necessary to remove some of the beauty and riches of the earth from his sight and grasp.

(3) "Mercy had ceased its pleading for the guilty race. The beasts of the field and the birds of the air had entered the place of refuge. Noah and his household were within the ark; *'and the Lord shut him in.'* A flash of light was seen, and a cloud of glory, more vivid than the lightning, descended from heaven, and hovered before the entrance of the ark. The massive door, which it was impossible for those within to close, was slowly swung to its place by unseen hands. Noah was shut in, and the rejecters of God's mercy were shut out. The seal of heaven was on that door; God had shut it, and God alone could open it.

(4) "Upon the eighth day, dark clouds overspread the heavens. There followed the muttering of thunder and the flash of lightning. Soon large drops of rain began to fall. The world had never witnessed anything like this, and the hearts of men were struck with fear....Then *'the fountains of the great deep [were] broken up, and the windows of heaven were opened.'* Water appeared to come from the clouds in

mighty cataracts. Rivers broke from their boundaries, and overflowed the valleys. Jets of water burst from the earth with indescribable force, throwing massive rocks hundreds of feet into the air, and these, in falling, buried themselves deep in the ground" (*Patriarchs and Prophets* 98-99).

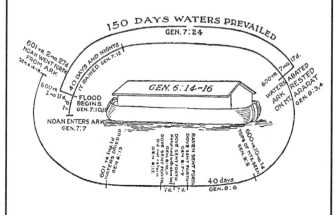

Lesson IV
The Drying of the Waters

Study Genesis 8.

Readings: Psalm 78:26; 148:8; 104:6-9; Nahum 1:3-6; Jonah 1:4; *Patriarchs and Prophets*, Chapter 8

Spelling Words: dove, savour, abate, restrain, Ararat, altar, raven, harvest decrease, asswaged

Memory Verse: *"The Lord smelled a sweet savour; and the Lord said in his heart, I will not again curse the ground any more for man's sake"* (Genesis 8:21).

Review:

1. What did God cause to blow to dry up the waters?

2. Describe the drying up of the waters.

3. Where did the ark rest? When?

4. When were the tops of the mountains seen?

5. What did Noah first send forth from the ark?

6. What did he next send? Why did the dove return?

7. When did Noah and his family come out of the ark?

8. How long had they been in the ark?

9. What was Noah's first act after coming out of the ark?

10. What promise did the Lord make to him?

11. What did He say should never cease while the earth remains?

Notes: (1) We may now use a map with our lessons. Why?

(2) What evidence of a universal flood does the earth itself give?

(3) Make a list of the effects, or results, of the Flood.

(4) Can you now explain the origin of coal fields, oil wells, volcanoes, mountain ranges, valleys, and the ocean?

(5) "The entire surface of the earth was changed at the Flood. A third dreadful curse rested upon it in consequence of sin. As the water began to subside, the hills and mountains were surrounded by a vast, turbid sea. Everywhere were strewn the dead bodies of men and beasts. The Lord would not permit these to remain to decompose and pollute the air, therefore He made the earth a vast burial-ground. A violent wind which was caused to blow for the purpose of drying up the waters, moved them with great force, in some instances even carrying away the tops of the mountains, and heaping up trees, rocks, and earth above the bodies of the dead. By the same means the silver and gold, the choice wood and precious stones, which had enriched and adorned the world before the Flood, and which the inhabitants had idolized, were concealed from the sight and search of men, the violent action of the waters piling earth and rocks upon these treasures, and in some cases even forming mountains above them" (*Patriarchs and Prophets* 107-108).

(6) "The earth presented an appearance of confusion and desolation impossible to describe. The mountains, once so beautiful in their perfect symmetry, had become broken and irregular. Stones, ledges, and ragged rocks were now scattered upon the surface of the earth. In many places, hills and mountains had disappeared, leaving no trace where they once stood; and plains had given place to mountain ranges. These changes were more marked in some places than in others. Where once had been earth's richest treasures of gold, silver, and precious stones, were seen the heaviest marks of the curse. And upon countries that were not inhabited, and those where there had been the least crime, the curse rested more lightly.

(7) "At this time immense forests were buried. These have since been changed to coal, forming the extensive coal beds that now exist, and also yielding large quantities of oil. The coal and oil frequently ignite and burn beneath the surface of the earth. Thus rocks are heated, limestone is burned, and the iron ore melted. The action of the water upon the lime adds fury to the intense heat. As the fire and water come in contact with ledges of rock and ore, there are loud explosions, and volcanic eruptions follow. These often fail of giving sufficient vent to

the heated elements, and the earth itself is convulsed, the ground opens, and villages, cities, and burning mountains are swallowed up" (*Patriarchs and Prophets* 108).

Lesson V
The Bow of Promise

Study Genesis 9:1-19.

Readings: Ezekiel 1:28; Isaiah 54:9-10; Revelation 4:2-3; *Patriarchs and Prophets,* Chapter 8

Spelling Words: herb, fear, token, covenant, perpetual, bow, flesh, require, replenish, overspread

Memory Verse: *"I do set my bow in the cloud, and it shall be for a token of a covenant between me and the earth"* (Genesis 9:13).

Review:
1. How did God further recognize Noah's offering?

2. How was man to be regarded by the animals?

3. What food was man now given permission to eat?

4. What restriction was made in the eating of flesh? Why? Leviticus 17:10-11

5. What value is placed upon the life of a man?

6. What is a covenant?

7. What everlasting covenant was made with all flesh?

8. What is the token of the covenant? Where is it seen?

9. What is a token?

10. By how many persons was the whole earth overspread, or peopled?

11. How long did Noah live after the Flood? Genesis 9:28-29

Notes: (1) Of what is the rainbow around God's throne a token?

(2) Draw a rainbow, name its colors, and tell how it is produced.

(3) Before man sinned, the animals had no fear of man. They loved and obeyed him; but after sin entered the world, their nature became wild and fierce. To protect the life of man, they were made to fear and dread him. Even yet, however, when they are kindly treated, many of them lose their fear, and learn to love and trust their human friends.

(4) "It was God's purpose that as the children of after-generations should

ask the meaning of the glorious arch which spans the heavens, their parents should repeat the story of the Flood, and tell them that the Most High had blended the bow, and placed it in the clouds as an assurance that the waters should never again overflow the earth.

(5) "When man by his great wickedness invites the divine judgments, the Saviour, interceding with the Father in his behalf, points to the bow in the clouds, to the rainbow around the throne and above His own head, as a token of the mercy of God to the repentant sinner" (*Patriarchs and Prophets* 106-107).

The Rainbow

The rainbow, how glorious it is in the sky,
And yet its bright colors are soft to the eye;
There violet, blue, and bright yellow are seen,
And orange, and red, and most beautiful green.

Oh, I wonder what paints the bright bow in the sky.
See, it spreads out so wide, and it arches so high.
But now at one end 'tis beginning to fade,
And nothing is seen but a cloud's misty shade.

'Tis God who thus paints the fair heavenly bow,
And sets it on high, His great mercy to show;
He bids men look on it, and then call to mind
His promise once graciously made to mankind.

The sea, it may swell, and the clouds roll on high,
But God rules the sea, and the wild, stormy sky;
And ever henceforth shall the sea its bounds know,
Nor o'er the dry land in a wild deluge flow.

Then, when in the sky is the wide spanning bow,
It shall teach me God's goodness and mercy to know;
And that glorious God it shall teach me to love,
Who paints His great mercy in colors above.

A Christian's Alphabet

A – Adopted into the household of faith

B – Born from above

C – Chosen of God in love

D – Dead to the world

E – Elected by grace

F – Forgiven of God

G – Glorified in heaven

H – Holy in Christ

I – Immortality of life

J – Justified by faith

K – King under Christ

L – Living in the Light

M – Merciful, obtaining mercy

N – New creature in Christ

O – Obedient servant

P – Patient in suffering

Q – Quickened from the dead

R – Redeemed by the precious blood of Christ

S – Saved by grace

T – Transformed into His likeness

U – Unspotted from the world

V – Vigilant for the truth

W – Workman that need not be ashamed

X – 'Xample of God's grace

Y – Yielding unto God

Z – Zealous in good works

The Alphabet and the Rainbow

The colors of the rainbow come from light. So when God said *"let there be light"* (Genesis 1:3), He was also saying "let there be color." What does it mean then when Jesus said, *"I am the light of the world?"* (John 8:12) We know He is like a light giving spiritual understanding to guide us in the pathway of life. Since color can represent character this Light gives us awareness of our character needs.

Have you heard the statement "never be ashamed to display your colors," or who you represent? By our character we demonstrate whose banner we are serving under, prince Immanuel or the arch deceiver.

Jesus said, *"I am Alpha and Omega"* or the alphabet of the Word of God which teaches us how to attain character development.

The word alphabet comes to us from the Greek language, and is made up to the first two letters of the Greek alphabet, alpha and beta. However, we do not get our alphabet so directly from the Greek nation as we get the word alphabet. No one really knows all about where our alphabet did come from.

It grew very slowly, like all the other great works of civilizations. No one clever man sat down and wrote out the alphabet of any language. It is not the product of one man's mind, but the slow growth of the minds of many men.

The letters of our alphabet are called Roman. But the Romans did not invent it. It had been growing for many thousands of years before them. They only put the finishing touches on it.

The first alphabet was made up of pictures; for people wrote by pictures long before they did by the signs of sounds. That is what letters are—the signs of sounds. The letter O was at first just the picture of an eye; and it was made simpler and simpler until it grew to be only a plain circle and became the letter O. The letter L was at first the picture of a man standing; and the letter A was the picture of a house or pyramid. We do not know all the pictures and how they were changed.

What sign or picture is the rainbow to remind us of? Our covenant* relationship with God.

*an agreement of two

Some of the earliest alphabets were developed by the Egyptians, the Semites, the Phoenicians, the Cypriots, and the Greeks. God through the alphabet prepared the way for Moses to begin the writing of the Scriptures. He fled from Egypt to Midian. There under the inspiration of the Holy Spirit, he wrote the books of Genesis and Job.

The alphabet as it now stands is a very wonderful thing. As I sit here in my home, and write these words, I know that by and by you will sit in your home and read them, and be able to understand me just as if I were talking to you. I feel very grateful for the alphabet.

When observing the rainbow in the sky we know God is speaking to us. He is reminding us that we have *"made a covenant"* with Him (Deuteronomy 5:2).

After we learn the alphabet, we begin at once to learn to form words by combining the different letters and the sounds they represent. We go on doing this as long as we live; but no one person ever knows all the words in any language, to say nothing of all the other languages in the world.

Likewise we learn to mix colors to make new ones, such as yellow and blue to make green.

An authority on alphabets once said that if we took an alphabet of twenty-four letters—and some have just that number—these letters might be arranged in 620,448,401, 733,239,439,340,000 different ways, though I, for my part, do not know how he ever worked that all out. I am very sure that he never made so many words in his own lifetime. In fact, he himself says that he did not. And, more than that, it would take all the people in the world, each writing forty pages a day, with forty sets of letters to the page, more than a million years to write so many words. Is that a task to think about! I am very glad we do not have to do it. All the people in the world writing at once would be very uninteresting.

It is estimated that we can distinguish as many as 10 million colors. Each color differs from all others in some degree of hue, lightness, or chroma.* All these colors come from the seven colors of the rainbow.

Colors have meaning for we say, "he is blue" which means sad, or "do not be a yellow belly" which means a coward.

*the purity of a color, determined by its degree of freedom from white or gray; color intensity

The Scriptures teach us what colors mean as they teach us what words mean in heaven's language.

One person wrote a poem describing color relating to Christ.

A rainbow round the throne I see,
It meaneth much to you and me;
The red is symbol of Christ's blood,
That touches, cleanses sin's dark flood,
    And saves the soul.

The blue reminds us of the blow
That bruised Christ's cheek when
                 here below:
The green, the freshness of the grace
That gives a glory to the face
    Of him who prays.

Humility, the violet—
Above all the arch in colors set,
Above man's hatred, far above,
Shines forth a symbol of God's love,
    Oh Saviour mine!

Oh bow of promise, circling there
Around the throne in colors fair,
O let thy glory be unfurled
Forever o'er our little world!
    O Jesus come!
        —E. H. Morton

New words, though, are most interesting. When we have learned a new word, it is good to learn something about how it grew, and exactly what it means now, and what it meant when the word was first used. It is also important to learn how to spell it correctly.

Colors can be studied so that you may discover interesting ideas about them. For instance, colors affect people.

    Red is a stimulating color.
    Orange is an action color.
    Yellow is a cheerful color.
    Green is a restful color.
    Blue is a reserved color.
    Purple is a royal color.

The letters of the alphabet appear generally in a similar order in nearly all languages; but just how they came to be in this order no one really knows. The English and German alphabets have twenty-six letters each; the French, 25; Spanish, 27; Italian, 20; Russian, 36; Greek, 24; Latin and Hebrew, each 22; Celtic, 17; Arabic, 28; Persian, 31; Turkish, 28; Sanskrit, 44; Chinese, 214.

A rainbow always shows its colors in an exact order: red, orange, yellow, green, blue, indio, and violet. When there is a double rainbow, the second will reverse that order.

In all languages the alphabet is imperfect, and one letter often has to stand for two or more sounds. In the English language, for instance, there are forty-two sounds and only twenty-six letters, and some of those are only repetitions of the same sounds. There is no sound for the letter C that could not be represented by the letter S or the letter K. The sound of Ch though is distinct, and yet it has no single letter to cover it. Its sound bears no relation to either the sound of C or H.

There is one verse in the Bible that contains all the letters in the English alphabet except the letter J: and that letter used to be the same as the letter I. It is the twenty-first verse of the seventh chapter of Ezra.

> "And I, even I Artaxerxes the king, do make a decree to all the treasures which are beyond the river, that whatsoever Ezra the priest, the scribe of the law of the God of heaven, shall require of you, it be done speedily."
> Ezra 7:21

Look for all the colors of the rainbow in the Scriptures.

There are two English words that contain all the vowels of our language and in their proper order. These words are facetious* and abstemious.** There are at least eighteen other words in our language that contain all the vowels, but not in their proper order.

*playfully jocular; humorous and flippant **sparing in diet; refraining from strong drink

Look in nature for things of creation that shows all the colors of the rainbow. Can you find anything that has all the colors in order?

There is hardly to be found a more interesting game for both young and old people than the choosing of a number of letters and trying to see how many different words may be formed with them. The same can be done with the mixing of colors.

Alphabet blocks are usually one of the first play things given to a child; and we feel very happy when he has learned A or B though it seems to us by that time a very simple thing to learn. It is not such a simple thing though: for it is the foundation of all the learning in the world, and the use of words in a study that has fascinated the minds of the great scholars. The elements of all the words are found right on the baby's blocks. So are all colors found in a simple rainbow.

Rebus

A rebus is a message composed of words or syllables depicted by symbols or pictures that suggest the sound of the words or syllables they represent. This is like the early beginnings of the written language.

Fill in the proper words in each blank and read the rebus message.

"Cause To Sit"

M +

"_____ _____ _____ _____

_____ _____ _____,

AND _____ + T   SH + ALL _____ FOR A TOKEN

OF A _____ _____ + T + WEEN ME AND

THE _____ _____." Genesis 9:13

Spelling and the Alphabet

There are 26 letters in the alphabet which we use to spell the more than 700,000 words of the English language. These words have come from virtually every civilized tongue.

Spelling is the way we combine letters to form words. Learning to spell correctly is part of learning to master the English language. The art and study of spelling is called orthography.*

"Orthography
is so absolutely necessary
for a man of letters,
or a gentleman,
that one false spelling may fix
a ridicule upon him
for the rest of his life."
—Lord Chesterfield

Let all the foreign tongues alone
Till you can **spell** and read your own.
—Isaac Watts

*the art or study of correct spelling according to established usage

Alpha and Omega

"I am Alpha and Omega,
the beginning and the ending..."
Revelation 1:8

What is God like?

Who would have thought, if it had not been told us, that He was like the letters in the alphabet? In the Greek alphabet in which the New Testament was written, Alpha was the first letter and Omega was the very last letter. So, in effect God is saying "I am A and Z."

There is a little Chinese toy, which consists of five pieces of wood; shaped so as to fit each other in a variety of ways. And out of those five little bits of wood you can form two or three thousand different shapes; arrange the pieces differently, and you have a different shape.

But although that is a very wonderful toy, it is not to be compared to the alphabet. You can arrange the few letters of the alphabet into thousands upon thousands of different words. And no new word could arise for which, if we use the whole alphabet, we could not find a shape or word to express it.

A A A A–Z Z Z Z

All that we speak, then, all that we write, all that ever has been written, all that ever will be written, you will find enclosed in the twenty-six letters of the alphabet.

Now that is why this is the name of God. God says, "I am like the alphabet; I am its first letter, I am its last letter, and I am all the letters between."

As all language in all the world in the A, B, C, so all life, all power, and all goodness are to be found in God.

But here we have only this first and last letter.

He is the beginning and the end of your life. He is the Maker of it. It is made for His glory. He is the beginning and end of all religion in the life. He is the Author and Finisher.

Two thoughts come to us here: Where did my religion come from? It came from God. What did I receive my religion for? To serve God.

Now another way to understand is this: What should be your first thought in the morning? It should be God! What should be your last thought at night? God!

What should be your first concern in life? To please God. What should be your last? Have I pleased God?

The happy life is the life that, looking back, sees God in childhood and the life that is closing, resting in God until He comes again to take all home to heaven with Him.

—Adapted From
The Child Jesus

Unique Alphabet of the Bible

**Rewrite the verse for C* and R*
using the words covenant and rainbow.**

A is for Adam, who was the first man;
   He broke God's commands, and thus sin began.
                     Genesis 3

B is the Book which to guide is given;
   Though written by man, the words came from Heaven.
                     II Peter 1:20-21

C* is for Christ, who for sinners was slain;
   By Him, Oh, how freely salvation we gain!
                     John 3:16

D is for Dove with an olive leaf green;
   Returning in peace to the ark she is seen.
                     Genesis 8:11

E is for Elijah, whom, by the brookside,
   Daily with food the ravens supplied.
                     I Kings 17:4

F is for Felix, who sent Paul away,
   And designed to repent on some future day.
                     Acts 24:25

G is for Goliath—lo! stretched on the plain,
   By the sling of young David, the giant is slain.
                     I Samuel 17:49

H is for Hannah, how happy is she!
   Her son, little Samuel, how holy was he!
                     I Samuel 1:20; 2:26

I is for Isaac, like Jesus, he lies
   Stretched out on the wood a meek sacrifice.
                     Genesis 22:1-13

J is for Joseph, who trusted God's Word;
   Was lifted from prison to be Egypt's lord.
                              Geneis 41:40-44

K is for Korah; God's wrath he defined,
   And lo! to devour him the pit opened wide.
                              Numbers 16:30-33

L is for Lydia; God opened her heart,
   What He had bestowed, it was her joy to impart.
                              Acts 16:14-15

M is for Mary, who fed on Christ's word,
   And Martha, her sister, beloved of the Lord.
                              Luke 10:38-42

N is for Noah; with God for his guide,
   Safely he sails o'er the billowy tide.
                              Genesis 7:17-18

O is for Obakiah, who, the prophets to save,
   Twice fifty concealed and fed in a cave.
                              I Kings 18:4

P is for Peter, who walked on the wave,
   But, sinking, he cried, "Lord, I perish: Oh save!"
                              Matthew 14:24-30

Q is for Queen, who from distant land came,
   Allured by the sound of King Solomon's fame.
                              I Kings 10:1-10

R* is for Ruth; she goes forth mid the sheaves,
   Gleaning the ears the husbandman leaves.
                              Ruth 2:23

S is for Stephen, Christ's martyr who cried
   To God for his murderers and then died.
                              Acts 7:51-60

T is for Timothy, taught in his youth
   To love and to study the Scriptures of truth.
                              II Timothy 3:15

U is for Uzziah, in rashness and pride
　Profaning God's altar, a leper he died.
　　　　　　　II Chronicles 26: 16, 21

V is for Vine; a green branch may I be,
　Bearing fruit to the glory of Jesus, the Tree.
　　　　　　　John 15:1

W is for Widow, her two mites she gave,
　And trusted in God to sustain her and save.
　　　　　　　Mark 12:41-44

X is the Cross our dear Saviour bore;
　Oh, think of His sorrows, and grieve Him no more.
　　　　　　　John 19:17

Y is for Youth Eutychus, killed by a fall;
　By a miracle wrought was recovered by Paul.
　　　　　　　Acts 20:9-12

Z is for Zoar, where Lot wished to be,
　It reminds me of Christ a refuge for me
　　　　　　　Genesis 19:22

 Something About Color

It was a rainy day in spring. A long, long, weary day it had been to Herbert. It was not easy for an active little boy to stay in the house all day.

"Girls don't seem to care," said Herbert. "But, really, Mamma, it makes my very bones ache to stay in the house all day. Do you think it will rain tomorrow?"

Herbert sat looking out of the window with longing eyes. Mamma laid aside her sewing and took a seat near him.

"I think tomorrow will be a fair day," she said cheerily. "See, the clouds are breaking away now!"

In a moment more the sun burst forth in all its glory. It shone so brightly that Herbert almost wondered where the rain could come from.

"Oh, Mamma, there's a rainbow! Isn't it beautiful! I don't believe I ever saw a brighter one. See, there's another one! Two beautiful rainbows!" exclaimed Herbert. He was too excited to sit still. He danced for joy. At last he turned a somersault in the middle of the room. Nothing else seemed quite so fitting an expression of his feelings.

"May I go outdoors now, Mamma?" he asked. "Just as soon as it stops raining," replied his mother. "But while it continues to rain, let us have a little talk about this beautiful rainbow. Do you know when the first rainbow was seen?"

"Oh, yes, Mamma. It was when Noah came out of the ark."

"Yes, my child. The rainbow was God's promise to Noah that never again would He destroy the earth with a flood. All the rainbows that have ever been seen since then are really God's way of telling us that He will save us, if we will obey Him as Noah did. The Bible tells us that there is a beautiful rainbow about God's throne in heaven. Every rainbow should cause us to think of God and heaven. It should cause us to be very grateful that He has done so much for us."

"Maybe that is why everyone is so glad to see the rainbow, Mamma. But what makes the different colors?"

"What colors do you see in it?" asked Mamma.

"There are red, orange, yellow, green, blue, and violet."

"Every raindrop acts just like the prism you were playing with the other day. Don't you remember that it made the colors of the rainbow when the sun shone through it? All these different colors are found in the sunlight. As it shines through the raindrops, the light is broken up into all the colors. As each ray of light enters the raindrop, it is bent out of its straight path. The red color is bent less than the others. Each of the others in its turn is bent a little more than the one before it. The colors of the rainbow are found everywhere in nature. Did you ever stop to think why some flowers are blue while others are red?"

"No, Mamma; why is it?"

"A flower looks blue when the blue rays of the light are sent back from it to your eyes. All the other colors are shut up in the flower. No one knows how this is done. It is one of the Lord's wonders. A red flower sends back the red rays to our eyes, and keeps all the other colors. A white flower sends back every color, for white is a mixture of all the colors. Anything that is black sends back none of the colors, for black is an absence of all color. A white dress is cooler than a black one, because it does not take up any of the colors from the sunlight, but sends them all away from itself.

Black cloth, when wet, will dry sooner than white cloth of the same kind. Can you tell why this is?"

"I suppose it must be because the colors in the sunlight are all held in the black cloth and all sent away from the white."

"Yes, that is exactly the reason. And for the same reason water heats more quickly in a black kettle than it does in a light-colored one. And a magnifying glass will set fire to black paper before it will white paper. But while we have been talking, the rain has ceased, the clouds have disappeared, and my little boy has time for a frolic with Rover."

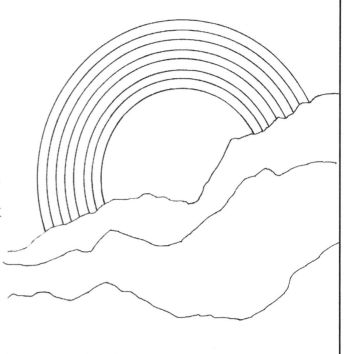

Review
Use the ideas below when the student reads a story.

Discussion

1. What makes the colors of the rainbow?

2. What does the rainbow say?

3. Where is the rainbow in heaven?

4. Name the colors of the rainbow in their order.

5. Which color always comes on top of the bow?

6. Why are some flowers blue?

7. Why are some things black? white?

8. Why is a white dress cooler than a black one?

9. In what kind of kettle will water boil sooner, a black or a light-colored one? Why?

10. Which kind of paper will burn first under a glass, black or white? Why?

Sentence Study

11. How many sentences in paragraph one and two? Read those that make statements; those that ask questions. Read an exclamation in paragraph four.

12. Read this story leaving out everything except the exact words of the speakers. Notice the quotation marks; they will help you to know what parts to read.

Written Exercise

13. In complete sentences, write answers to as many as you can of the questions under "Discussion." Number your answers, write neatly, and be careful of spelling, capitals, and punctuation marks.

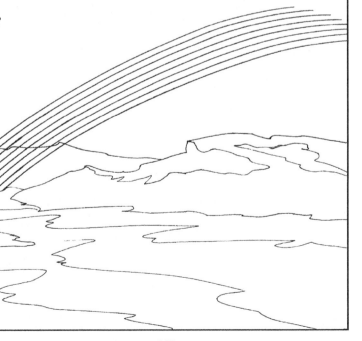

The
First Grade

First Grade

A Good Reading Program

Recommendations

We recommend that the student spend the first year of formal schooling learning Bible, nature-science, character development, and how to read, write, spell, and other simple English skills.

Use the Bible as the child's first reader. There are many simple nature books that also make good reading books.

Once this foundation is securely laid in language skills, the child is ready for mathematics, history, geography, music, and other academic subjects

The student usually does much better if he begins his "close" work of reading and writing at an older age.

Writing and Spelling Road to Reading and Thinking (WSRRT)

Have you ever gone to a church fellowship dinner? Afterwards perhaps you have had indigestion from too many varieties of food at one meal. As with the delicate stomach, so it is with the young mind when we give it too large a variety of thought patterns at once. "Teach one idea and teach it well," is a motto that we would do well to heed.

We have found that students just beginning their book work do best by only learning the following subjects: Bible, Nature, and WSRRT that first grade. While learning to read, the Bible will become the child's reader. It is far more valuable to read, *"In the beginning God,"* than some meaningless words.

We recommend that the first grade student spend one **full** year in WSRRT, or longer if necessary, before going on to other academic subjects. A good reader, writer, speller, and speaker usually excels quickly in all other classes.

Because they lack in the area of reading and spelling, many high school and college students have poor habits of learning. Many have had to go back to the very beginning. They can use the WSRRT but do it in a shorter period of time in a more mature fashion. But think of the years of inhibited learning because they did not have this foundation.

Noah had a blueprint to use in building the ark. So in language we need the "blueprint" to build correctly.

This course helps the student in all areas of his life. For example, it helps a student to be neat and tidy, do perfect work, and to persevere in difficult tasks.

When the beginning student has mastered the WSRRT, proceed on to the other academic subjects, such as mathematics and history.

If you have a student who has difficulties in reading, writing, or spelling, contact SonLight to speak to a qualified person about this matter.

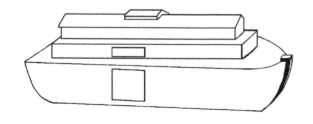

At the Point of the Pen

"There, Ruth, how you startled me! Sit down dear: I was just reading over some of your college letters. You cannot imagine how much I have enjoyed them, especially since—"

"Since what?" demanded Ruth with an encouraging smile, as she laid her skates on the rug beside her.

"Since you took that course in penmanship," replied her aunt, with a loving glance at the envelope in her hand.

"My course in penmanship!" cried Ruth. "My dear Aunt Phoebe, no learned professor is responsible for the plain business hand that so delights you eye. I learned a little lesson last spring when college was closed during the epidemic in town. I took the last train home, hurried from the station, tiptoed up the steps, and stood for a moment outside the screen door watching the homelike scene within. Mother was reading a letter aloud:

" 'We had a-a s-c-r—' I don't know what that word is, Father, but some kind of a 'time in—' "

"Never mind," said Father; "you may be sure it was a good time if Ruth was in it."

"Scrumptious!" ejaculated Bobby, but Mother was reading on.

" 'Time in Rachel's room last night. I wrote you how mel-melon-melan-melancholy that young Professor Br–Bre–Bri—' "

"Call it Smith," suggested Father.

"Smith," continued Mother, "has been since her brother was killed in the battle of L–L—"

"Liege, Louvain," supplied Bobby.

" 'Louvain.' Thank you, Bobby. 'We didn't really want to invite her to our sp-spr-spread, but listened to the call of duty. She proud' no 'proved to be perfectly charming, as she showed us how to make French candy–the most delicate'–no 'delicious con-con-con-concoction I ever ate. Now all the girls have a er-ern—' "

"Yes, Aunt Phoebe, it was the sixteen-page letter I had sent out that week, and it had taken Mother three minutes to read one page. Father's head was beginning to nod, and Bobby had a studious eye on his geography.

" 'Now, Father, you go to sleep.' I heard Mother say, 'I'll make this out, and tell you all the news at the breakfast table.'

" 'Father opened his eyes, looked across the table at mother, and advised her not to 'puzzle out' the letter until morning: for she had been cleaning house all day, and must be tired.'

"That was enough. I burst into the house, seized my letter, and proceeded to read it dramatically, after explaining my unexpected arrival, of course. As I foundered over a dozen words, Bobby shouted, and father and mother sat there and smiled as if all their troubles were at an end."

"And you took a private course in penmanship?"

"Yes, at my own little desk, with myself as instructor," replied Ruth.

Build a Good Foundation

Lay the foundation in reading, writing, spelling, and speaking as securely as Noah built the ark with the very best of materials.

Spelling Basics

Spelling Basics

> "...A word spoken
> in due season,
> how good is it!"
> Proverbs 15:23

1. Hear It!
2. Say It!
3. Write It!
4. See It!

If you follow these 4 steps in order, spelling will become easier.
This section makes an excellent review after the student has had
a good foundation laid by the WSRRT.

How to Learn to Spell a Word

1. Hear the word pronounced.

2. Pronounce the word syllable by syllable.

3. Write the word. Look at the word and say it again. Take a clear mental picture of the word. Notice any double letters, silent letters, or other difficult parts.

4. Close your eyes and think how the word sounds and looks. See every letter, every syllable.

5. Find opportunities to use the word in your speaking and writing, and soon it will be mastered!

How to Avoid Misspelling Words

1. Master the lists of common words that are frequently misspelled found on pages 37 and 57.

2. Keep a list of the words you misspell in themes, letters, tests, and spelling exercises. You will find the list surprisingly short—perhaps not more than twenty-five words long, probably not more than a hundred.

3. Make it a habit to look up words in the dictionary unless you are certain that your spelling is correct.

4. After writing the first draft of a letter or report, search for spelling errors and correct them. Because spelling is largely a matter of visual memory, teach yourself to observe words sharply. When a word you write does not look right, it is usually wrong. Look it up in the dictionary.

Read the story, "The Little Girl and Her Copy" on page 35.

A Spelling Game

One-Word Story

The one-word story can be the most enjoyable indoor game imaginable if the players have plenty of imagination and native wit.

They sit in a circle, and one begins a story by writing just one word on a piece of paper. His neighbor gives the second word and this continues round and round the circle. Those players who cannot supply a word, or who use a word that does not make sense, must leave the circle.

The keenest part of the game comes when only two or three are left. The one who survives after all the others have left the circle will read the story out loud for the others to enjoy.

Reform Spelling

There is a farmer who is Y's
    Enough to take his E's
And study nature with his I's
    And think of what he C's

He hears the chatter of the J's
    As they each other T's
And C's that when a tree DK's
    It makes a home for B's

A yoke of oxen he will U's
    With many haws and G's
And their mistakes he will XQ's
    When plowing for his P's

He little buys, but much he sells,
    And therefore little O's
And when he hoes his soil by spells,
    He also soils his hose.

Hard Spots

Below find a list of the ten hardest words. The following are the ten words most frequently misspelled by students. The hard parts are underlined. Look carefully at these letters.

beli<u>e</u>ve   sep<u>a</u>rate
com<u>mittee</u>   therefor<u>e</u>
<u>its</u>   th<u>ei</u>r
pleas<u>a</u>nt   tog<u>e</u>ther
princip<u>a</u>l   t<u>oo</u>

Too is an adverb meaning excessive (as in "too tired") or also. **To** is a preposition meaning toward. **Two** is the number 2.

It's is a contraction of it is: "it's raining." **Its** is a possessive pronoun: "its trunk," "its branches."

Their is a possessive pronoun: "their home," "their Bibles." **There** is an adverb: "Put the book there;" "Is there any rain?"

The adjective **principal** means chief. The noun **principal** means head of a school, leader, or sum on which interest is paid. **Principle** is always a noun meaning law, truth, doctrine, or moral rule.

Exercises

I. As you write the following sentences, fill the blanks with too, to, or two.

1. Mankind had become ____ wicked and God decided ____ destroy that world with a flood.

2. The sky looked ____ clear for rain and nobody believed what Noah said would come ____ pass.

3. Noah was ____ take animals into the ark ____ by ____, male and female.

4. God would use these ____ of each kind to repopulate the earth after the Flood.

5. When it began ____ rain, people remembered what Noah had said, but it was ____ late.

The Little Girl and Her Copy

A girl went to writing school. When she saw her copy, with every line so perfect, she said, "I can never write like that."

She looked steadfastly at the straight round lines so slim and graceful. Then she took up her pen, and timidly put it on the paper. Her hand trembled; she stopped, studied the copy, and began again. "I can but try," said the girl; "I will do as well as I can."

She wrote half a page. The letters were crooked. What more could we expect from a first effort? The next scholar stretched across her desk and said, "What scraggy things you make!" Tears filled the girl's eyes. She dreaded to have the teacher see her book. "He will be angry with me and scold," she said to herself.

But when the teacher came and looked, he smiled. "I see you are trying," he said kindly, "and that is enough for me."

She took courage. Again and again she studied the beautiful copy. She wanted to know how every line went, how every letter was rounded and made. Then she took up her pen, and began to write. She wrote carefully, with the copy always before her. But oh, what slow work it was! Her letters straggled here, they crowded there, and some of them looked every way.

The girl trembled at the step of the teacher. "I am afraid you will find fault with me," she said; "my letters are not fit to be on the same page with the copy."

"I do not find fault with you," said the teacher, "because I do not look so much at what you do. By really trying, you make a little improvement every day; and a little improvement every day will enable you to reach excellence by-and-by.

"Thank you sir," said the girl; and thus encouraged, she took up her pen with a greater spirit of application than before.

And so it is with the dear children who are trying to become like Jesus. God has given us a heavenly copy. He has given us His dear Son "for an example, that we should follow His steps." He *did no sin, neither was guile found in his mouth"* (I Peter 2:22). *"He is altogether lovely,"* and *"full of grace and truth"* (Song of Solomon 5:16, John 1:14). And when you study His character, you say, "I can never, never reach that, I can never be like Jesus."

God does not expect you to become like His dear Son in a minute, or a day, or a year; but what pleases Him is that you should love Him, and try every day to follow His example. It is that disposition which helps you to grow day by day, little by little, into His likeness, which God desires to see. God loves you for trying, and will help you.

II. As you write the following sentences, fill each blank with its or it's.

1. When God told Noah, "_____ time," Noah and his family went into the ark and God closed ____ door.

2. _____ sad that the world had become so corrupt that _____ only inhabitants spared were Noah and his family.

3. But _____ encouraging that God spared _____ righteous, even when they were few.

4. God had Noah fill the ark with animals and _____ storage rooms with supplies.

5. _____ clear God's plan was complete, and _____ every detail was perfect.

III. As you write the following sentences, insert their or there in each blank.

1. _____ were lots of people who placed _____ faith in themselves instead of God.

2. _____ were two of every animal.

3. _____ was rain for forty days; and for more than 200 days _____ only view was water.

4. Noah sent out a raven and a dove to see if _____ was any dry land to be _____ resting place.

5. Finally Noah and his wife and _____ children were able to leave the ark when _____ was dry ground.

IV. Write the following sentences, filling each blank with principle or principal.

1. An important _____ we can learn from Noah is to not let other people's mocking keep us from obeying God.

2. One of Noah's _____ responsibilities was to build the ark according to God's plan.

3. The school _____ gave the _____ address on the story of Noah and the Flood.

4. God's promise to never destroy the world by flood again is a precious _____.

5. The _____ way God reminds us of His promise is through the rainbow.

Twenty Hard Words

acquaintance
all right
anyone
anything
benefit
business
dependent
everything
grammar
immediately

independent
meant
necessary
night
occurred
possessive
received
there
until
writing

All right, just as *all wrong*, is two words.

Contractions

Contractions are used freely in friendly letters, poems, stories, and conversation. In forming contractions, never add a letter and never change the order of the letters. Just put an apostrophe where one or more letters are left out.

Examples
are + not = aren't
it + is = it's
can + not = can't
(two letters omitted)
you + have = you've
(two letters omitted)
will + not = won't
(a peculiar contraction)
of + the + clock = o'clock

V. What words are combined to form each contraction? Write in parentheses the letter or letters omitted in the contraction.

Example
you'd = you would
(*woul* omitted)

couldn't _____   shouldn't _____

didn't _____   that's _____

doesn't _____   there's _____

don't _____   wasn't _____

hasn't _____   we'll _____

haven't _____   weren't _____

I'll _____   we've _____

I've _____   wouldn't _____

mustn't _____   you'll _____

she's _____   you're _____

VI. Prepare to write the following sentences at your teacher's dictation.

1. The door wasn't closed and the rains didn't fall until all were safely aboard the ark.

2. We mustn't doubt God's word, just as Noah didn't.

3. We'll always remember God's promise if we don't forget to look for the rainbow.

4. The animals wouldn't have come to the ark if God hadn't made them.

5. Noah knew the dove couldn't find a resting place when she returned to the ark.

6. I've heard of floods, but there's never been one worldwide like this one.

7. Noah and his family weren't out of the ark long before Noah offered sacrifices of thanksgiving.

8. Shouldn't we think about Noah and the Flood when we're in a rainstorm?

9. That's why we've been told to learn from the examples of the stories in the Bible.

10. You're sure to remember that Noah's sons were Shem, Ham, and Japheth.

11. Some people haven't stopped to think how big the ark must have been.

Using Hard Words

VII. Write sentences containing at least five of the Ten Hardest Words, five of the Twenty Hard Words, and ten or more contractions. You may use two or three in one sentence.

**Biblical Endings—
-el, -aid, -ayed, -o**

Several common words end in el, aid, and have o in them. Make a list of Bible verses containing them.

Some words that end in -el.

VIII. Dictate the Bible references to practice these words.

Abel – Genesis 4:2, 4; Hebrews 11:4
angel – Psalm 34:7
Bethel – Genesis 35:1
bowels – Lamentations 2:11
channel – Psalm 18:15; Isaiah 27:12
Daniel – Daniel 1:8
gravel – Proverbs 20:17
jewel – Proverbs 20:15;
        Isaiah 61:10; Malachi 3:17
minstrel – II Kings 3:15
Nathanael – John 1:45-49
Rachel – Genesis 29:10
rebel – Numbers 14:9
Samuel – I Samuel 1:20
shekel – Exodus 30:24
shovel – Isaiah 30:24
towel – John 13:4-5

Some words ending in -aid.

afraid – Genesis 3:10;
     Deuteronomy 31:6; Psalm 3:6
laid – Isaiah 51:13
maid – Matthew 9:24-25
paid – Jonah 1:3
said – Genesis 1:3

    Most verbs ending in -ay form the past tense by adding -ed. Words ending with the letter -a are not pronounced with the long $\bar{a}$ sound [except for the article a and less used words like yea and qua]. Words ending with the long $\bar{a}$ sound generally end with -ay or -ey unless they are foreign.

Examples

lay, delay, survey, convey,
bouquet, papermache

---

delayed – Exodus 32:1
played – I Samuel 18:10
stayed – Isaiah 26:3

    These words have a single -o in them.

forty – Genesis 7:4
move – Acts 17:28
prove – Psalm 26:2
whose – Psalm 32:1

Lose and Loose

    Lose is a verb meaning not to have any longer. **Loose** is usually an adjective meaning not tight. **Lose** is pronounced "looz;" **loose**, "loos."

loose – Isaiah 20:2; Luke 19:33
lose – Ecclesiastes 3:6;
    Matthew 10:39, 42; 16:25-26

IX. Fill each blank with loose or lose. Say the word aloud and then spell it correctly.

1. Their morals were so _____, they were to _____ their lives.

2. Noah tightened every joint so nothing on the ark was _____.

3. God planned to preserve life by the ark—Noah and those with him would not _____ hope.

4. No doubt every _____ item was tied down on the ark so they would not _____ anything in the wild storm.

5. We must be careful not to _____ control of our actions or _____ sight of God's law.

6. We can _____ proper focus under the influence of wine.

-ai, -oes, -os

X. These words have -ai in the last syllable. Dictate the Bible references to practice these words.

again – Psalm 126:1, 4, 6
against – Psalm 27:3, 12;
     Proverbs 24:28
captain – Joshua 5:14-15
certain – Daniel 1:3; Matthew 9:18;
     Matthew 18:23; 21:28, 33
complain – Lamentations 3:39;
     Numbers 11:1; Psalm 77:3
curtain – Numbers 3:26;
     Psalm 104:2; Isaiah 40:22
entertain – Hebrew 13:2
maintain – Psalm 140:12;
     Titus 3:8, 14
mountain – Exodus 19:3; 20:18;
     Song of Solomon 4:6;
     Isaiah 2:3; 11:9

Some frequently used plurals end in -oes.

heroes	Mosquitoes, potatoes and tomatoes only have **toes** when they are plural.
mosquitoes	
potatoes	
tomatoes	

Other plurals end in -os.

autos
pianos
radios
solos
sopranos

-ly and other doubling rules

Notice you add -ly to a word ending in -l.

cordial + ly = cordially

cruel + ly = cruelly

XI. Add -ly to each of the following words without losing an -l. Then write sentences to illustrate the use of five of these -ly words.

awful	final
beautiful	formal
cheerful	real
continual	regretful
cool	usual

On occasion a suffix or other syllable is added to a word ending in a single consonant preceded by a vowel. There are rules to guide us in the spelling.

A one-syllable word ending in a consonant preceded by one vowel doubles the final consonant when the suffix or other added syllable is a vowel or begins with one.

Each of the following examples shows how to spell both the original word and one of its derivatives.

Remember: (a) the original word has only one syllable; (b) it ends in a consonant preceded by one vowel; (c) the added ending begins with a vowel.

When a word of two or more syllables ends in a consonant preceded by one vowel and is accented on the last syllable, the final consonant is doubled before adding an ending beginning with a vowel.

Remember: (a) each word has more than one syllable; (b) each word ends with a consonant preceded by one vowel; (c) each word is accented on the final syllable; (d) each added final syllable begins with a vowel. We therefore double the final consonant of the word when we add another syllable. (There is one exception: crochet + ing = crocheting. This is because the final consonant is silent.)

When a word of two or more syllables ends in a consonant preceded by one vowel, but is not accented on the last syllable, the final consonant is not doubled before an added syllable that begins with a vowel.

Some words, such as bevel (beveled), imperil (imperiled), travel (traveled), counsel (counseled), and quarrel (quarreling), although not accented on the last syllable, may have the final consonant doubled before an added syllable beginning with a vowel, but the common practice today is not to double the final consonant. (For example: counsel + ed = counseled or counselled. But the preferred is counseled.)

In English we often double -l, -f, and -s following a single vowel at the end of a word of one syllable.

Examples	
err	will
shall	all
bell	kill
pass	miss
small	egg
full	add
fill	tell
class	ball
doll	call
fall	well

XII. The teacher may dictate words from the last 5 examples and the list below to test.

account	assure
accuracy	attempt
affair	dessert
allege	effect
apparent	marry
appears	millinery
appropriate	millionaire
artillery	official
arrangement	possess
arrest	pretty
arrive	scissors
assist	

-ceed, -cede, and -sede

When uncertain as to the spelling of words ending in -ceed, -cede, and -sede, consider that only three verbs belonging to this group end in -ceed—suceed, proceed, exceed. All others end in -ede. Such words as feed, deed, and weed are easy to spell correctly.

Examples	
-eed	**-ede**
exceed	accede
proceed	cede
succeed	concede
	intercede
	precede
	recede
	secede
	supersede

-or, -ar

Some words have endings in -or and -ar which sound just like -er.

-or

author	interior
color	janitor
director	labor
error	mirror
exterior	odor
favor	prior
harbor	radiator
honor	spectator
humor	superior
inferior	

-ar

beggar	particular
cedar	regular
cellar	scholar
dollar	vulgar

XIII. The following sentences are to be dictated by the teacher. Be careful of spelling, capitalization, and punctuation of these sentences.

1. Noah and his family are the heroes of the Bible story called the Flood.

2. It's all right for Noah to be dependent upon God for all his needs.

3. They didn't know He'd send a beautifully colored bow.

4. To face it continually raining for 40 days required unusual faith in God.

5. Noah's labor year after year helped him succeed in the job God gave him.

6. I wonder if some of the principal foods Noah took on the ark were tomatoes and potatoes.

7. Noah didn't complain about the rough trip.

8. Noah's family received a rainbow out of the cloudy curtain as a promise.

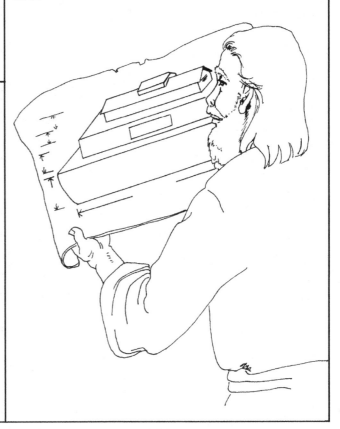

-ei, -ie

Place -i before -e except after -c, Or when sounded like "-a" as in neighbor and weigh.

Put -i before -e

achieve	mischievous
belief	niece
believe	piece
besiege	relief
cashier	relieve
chief	siege
handkerchief	wield

Except after -c

ceiling
conceive
deceit
deceive
perceive
receipt
receive

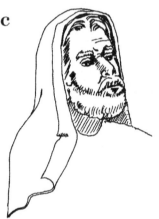

Or when sounded like "-a"

freight
neighbor
sleigh
veil
vein
weigh
weight

Exceptions

either
financier
foreign
forfeit
height
leisure
neither
seize
their
weird

Where -c is pronounced -sh, -ie follows the -c.

Examples	
ancient	efficient
conscience	sufficient

XIV. Fill in -ei and -ie for each word below.

anc___ nt

br ___ f

ch___ f

conc ___ t

consc ___ nce

dec ___ t

f ___ nd

f ___ rce

fr ___ ght

fr ___ nd

gr ___ f

gr ___ ve

h ___ ght

misch ___ f

n ___ ther

r ___ gn

rel ___ ve

sh ___ ld

shr ___ k

sl ___ gh

th ___ f

v ___ n

w ___ gh

w ___ght

y ___ ld

Review Silent -E Rules

1. The single vowels before any single consonant can say its name ("a," "e," "i," "o," or "u") if a silent -e follows to end the base word.

Examples
time (Tim)
here (her)
paste (past)
bathe (bath)

2. English words usually do not end with -v or the single vowel -u. An -e is added. (Exception: impromptu)

Examples
have
blue

3. The -e is added so -c and -g can say "s" and "j."

Examples
chance
charge

4. All syllables must contain at least one vowel. The silent -e in -ble, -cle, -dle, -fle, -gle, -kle, -ple, -sle, -tle, and -zle so they can be separate syllables.

Examples

little

humble

5. When the -e is not needed for any of the above reasons, it has no purpose.

Examples

are

come

house

promise

XV. Place a number by each word below to indicate which final silent -e rule applies.

1. Below are a list of words that might describe the wicked people before the Flood.

acquire __   fortune __
argue __   leisure __
associate __   nonsense __
broke rule __   persistence __
cause __   please __
dance __   pleasure __
deceive __   responsible __
desire __   stole __
ease __   terrible __
extreme __   trouble __
excuse __

2. These words could describe Noah and his family.

able __   prepare __
brave __   sensible __
courage __   separate __
gentle __   serve __
nice __   true __
organize __   reverence __
patience __   voice __
praise __   wholesome __
purpose __

3. What was the ark like and for?

accommodate __   outside __
architecture __   notice __
escape __   persevere __
expense __   possible __
inside __   serve __
house __   service __
large __   size __
immense __   sure __
invite __   vehicle __
move __

4. What did the earth look like after the Flood?

awe __   grave __
change __   icicle __
consequence __   precipice __
continue __   reprove __
disease __   undesirable __
fatigue __   waste __
freeze __

5. These words describe the rainbow.

above __	love __
blue __	orange __
circle __	peace __
declare __	picture __
exquisite __	promise __
hope __	shine __
life __	unchangeable __

6. What was the Flood like?

circle __	reprove __
circumference __	science __
complete __	strange __
entire __	surface __
fierce __	unfortunate __
impossible __	voyage __
noise __	

7. What went aboard the ark?

apple __	people __
article __	relative __
cabbage __	shoe __
eagle __	sleeve __
experience __	table __
evidence __	tissue __
goose __	tortoise __
horse __	treasure __
moose __	vegetable __
mouse __	

Final silent -e and suffixes

Words ending in a silent -e are usually simple to spell, but difficult when adding a suffix, such as -ing. For example, care + ing could be careing or caring. It is caring.

Final silent -e is usually dropped before a suffix beginning with a vowel.

Examples
appease + able = appeasable
blame + able = blamable
care + ing = caring
come + ing = coming
hate + ing = hating
plume + age = plumage

(Exceptions: hateable, agreeing, seeing, hoeing)

In words ending in -ie drop the -ie and add -y before a suffix beginning with a vowel.

Examples
die + ing = dying
lie + ing = lying
tie + ing = tying
vie + ing = vying

Final silent -e usually is retained before a suffix beginning with a consonant.

Examples

awe + some = awesome
care + less = careless
hoarse + ness = hoarseness
move + ment = movement
revenge + ful = revengeful

(Exceptions: awful, truly, duly, gently, judgment, wholly)

There are some exceptions to the preceding rule, most of them involving words containing -c and -g. In such words, keep the following information in mind:

Words ending in -ce or -ge usually retain the -e before a suffix beginning with -a or -o (so as to preserve the soft sound of the -c or -g).

Examples

trace + able = traceable
(Remember that -c in trace has the sound of -s—not -k.)

courage + ous = courageous
(The word is pronounced with a soft -g. In order to keep this sound, we keep the final -e.)

notice + able = noticeable
change + able = changeable
outrage + ous = outrageous
peace + able = peaceable
manage + able = manageable

In words where the suffix -ing is added, the final -c is given the hard sound, like that of -k; so therefore, it should not be followed by the vowel -i. In order to keep the -c from being pronounced -s, the letter -k is inserted, indicating that the -c is hard.

Examples

picnic + ing = picnicking
traffic + ing = trafficking
panic + y = panicky
mimic + ing = mimicking
frolic + ing = frolicking

A Game

Some Facts Concerning Our Kate (Cate)

This is an interesting game for young people, as it embodies most of the well-known words in the English language ending in cate. It would be well if the list were made out on a sheet of paper for each one taking part, the words guessed to be written down beside their respective numbers.

1. Kate is one of twins.

2. Kate is not strong.

3. Kate treats herself with medicine.

4. Kate uses oil on her hair.

5. Kate is good at finding places.

6. Kate shows the way.

7. Kate foretells events.

8. Kate is not always truthful.

9. Kate belongs to a trust.

10. Kate refuses to give up her position.

11. Kate justifies her action.

12. Kate may have her belongings seized.

13. Kate could involve others.

14. Kate had decided to leave the house where she is staying.

15. Kate's assistant was expelled from the church for heresy.

16. Kate has been allotted a share of her father's estate.

17. Kate chews her food well.

18. Kate at times shines brightly.

19. Kate makes up stories.

20. Kate uses ambiguous expressions.

21. Kate becomes confused.

22. Kate once put her shoulder out of joint.

23. Kate soon passes on news.

24. Kate teaches school.

25. Kate has given up her life to her work.

26. Kate sets her pupils perplexing problems.

27. Kate helps her pupils out of their difficulties.

28. Kate analyzes sentences.

29. Kate divides words into their component parts.

30. Kate's pupils sometimes dispute with one another.

31. Kate insills good principles into her pupils' minds.

32. Kate and her pupils have watched the drying of coconuts.

33. Kate's classes keep their school garden free from weeds.

34. Kate works faithfully against the use of those beverages that make people drunk.

Compounds

When writing compound numbers from twenty-one to ninety-nine use the hyphen.

Examples

twenty-two
twenty-four
fifty-one
sixty-five

Adjectives and Adverbs

A compound adjective consists of two or more words functioning as a unit before a noun.

Examples

well-built ship
first-class trip
five-quart bucket
two-family house
year-old bicycle
three-pound brick
high-ranking official
two-year-old girl

Do not hyphenate an adverb participle combination if the adverb ends in -ly.

poorly constructed house
highly valued employee
clearly defined laws

When these expressions occur elsewhere in the sentence, drop the hyphen if the individual words occur in a normal order and in a normal form.

an X-ray treatment = treated by X ray
up-to-date report = report up to date
high-level decision = made at high level

Before Noun	After Noun
worth-while book	This book is worth while.
near-by town	Is the town near by?
all-steel construction	The construction is all steel.
high-priced car	The car is high priced.

Points of the Compass

Points of the compass are written: northeast, southeast, northwest, southwest.

Pronouns

The following are compound pronouns: oneself, himself, themselves, ourselves, myself, herself, itself.

Anybody

Pronouns and adverbs ending with -body, -thing, and -where, such as anybody, are written without a hyphen or a space.

XVI. Write five pronouns or adverbs ending with -body, -thing, or -where.

One Word Compounds

Some words are so commonly used together that they have become words. They are written as one word without a hyphen or a space.

altogether
anyone
bathroom
bedroom
blackberries
bookkeeping
classroom
copyright
downstairs
everyone
forehead
foresee
grapefruit
heretofore
homework
indoors
mailbag
mailbox
mailman
mealtime
nevertheless

notebook
nowadays
outdoors
overcharge
postmaster
roommate
schoolboy
schoolroom
scrapbook
seaport
secondhand
semicolon
snowstorm
someone
sometime
therefore
throughout
typewriting
typewritten
upstairs
wastebasket

Exceptions

He will talk to **any one** of his students.

Every one of us enjoys seeing a rainbow.

The boat left **some time** ago.

The Prefix Self

Place a hyphen after the prefix -self: self-addressed, self-evident, self-explanatory, self-reliance, self-respect.

Prefixes

Prefixes joined to root words do not, as a rule, require the hyphen: nonpayment, semiannual, reinstate, international, overpay. A hyphen is used when the prefix is attached to a proper noun: all-American, un-American, un-Christian, pro-British.

Family

Usually hyphenate compounds of -father, -mother, -brother, -sister, -son, -daughter, and -great: father-in-law, sister-in-law, great-grand-mother.

Certain Words

      Hyphenate: ex-president, sight-seeing, good-by or good-bye.

Write as separate words.

all right	living room
dining room	no one
grape juice	parcel post (noun)
in spite of	

      The tendency is to write words solid. When in doubt, consult the dictionary.

XVII. The teacher can dictate the following sentences.

1. What did mealtime on the ark consist of? Did they have a dining room or did they eat in the bedroom?

2. Before the Flood, snowstorms and thunderstorms were unknown.

3. In the book of Revelation twenty-four elders see the rainbow around God's throne.

4. The lion and the lamb were shipmates on the eighty-six-foot wide ark. The height was fifty-two feet, while the length was five hundred fifteen feet.

5. How weary the occupants were to be indoors when they would have preferred to be outdoors.

6. Have you ever noticed the well-dressed mailman bringing mail to your mailbox on a rainy day?

7. I wonder if anyone did any bookkeeping while the ark was being built?

8. Some plants that went aboard the ark were grapes, blackberries, blueberries, and strawberries. That is why we have grape juice and berry pie today.

9. Noah had three sons and three daughters-in-law that chose to sail on the ship. Housecleaning was a full-time chore.

10. Sometime, in this large classroom, someone must have learned self-denial.

11. Noah had to be a shipbuilder, a preacher, a farmer, a provider, and a sailor.

12. The promises included even Noah's offspring, his unborn sons, and their wives, for at this time Noah was still childless.

Homonyms

Homonyms are words that sound alike but are spelled differently.

air (atmosphere)
heir (one who inherits)

aisle (a passageway)
isle (a small island)

allowed (permitted)
aloud (out loud)

altar (in church)
alter (to change)

assent (to agree)
ascent (act of rising)

bare (nude)
bear (to carry or an animal)

bass (a deep tone)
base (the bottom, or vile)

berth (on boat)
birth (of baby)

bough (branch of a tree)
bow (to bend)

break (to smash)
brake (a stopping device)

cannon (a large gun)
canon (a church law)

canvas (a stiff, heavy cloth)
canvass (to solicit)

capital (punishment)
Capitol (building where legislature
meets)

ceiling (the top of a room)
sealing (closing tightly)

cite (to quote)
site (location of something)
sight (ability to see)

claws (an animal's nails)
clause (part of a sentence)

coarse (rough)
course (of ship)

colonel (military rank)
kernel (part of nut or seed)

complement (that which completes)
compliment (flattering remark)

core (the center)
corps (a body of men)

council (group of lawmakers)
counsel (to give advice)

creek (small stream)
creak (squeak)

dear (highly valued)
deer (an animal)

dying (giving up life)
dyeing (coloring)

fair (just)
fare (transportation cost)

fir (a tree)
fur (coat of an animal)

forth (forward)
fourth (one of four parts)

hair (head covering)
hare (a rabbit)

hear (listen with your ear)
here (and there)

hole (in ground)
whole (complete)

lead (a metal)
led (past tense of lead, to guide)

lessen (to make less)
lesson (exercise studied)

meat (flesh)
meet (come together)

metal (iron, steel, copper)
mettle (strength of spirit)
medal (award, prize)

miner (one who mines)
minor (one under age)

pare (to peel)
pear (a fruit)

passed (past tense of pass)
past (adjective, gone by)

peace (state of quiet)
piece (a portion)

peel (to strip off)
peal (to ring)

peer (to look closely)
pier (a landing place)

plain (simple, not fancy)
plane (surface or aircraft)

pray (talk to God)
prey (an animal hunted by another)

rain (precipitation)
reign (rule)

raise (to lift)
raze (demolish)

right (correct)
rite (ritual)
write (put down words)

ring (a circle or a sound)
wring (to squeeze out)

road (highway)
rode (past tense of ride)

scene (place where something
          happens)
seen (past tense of see)

seem (appear)
seam (joining of two places)

serge (type of fabric)
surge (rush up)

shone (past tense of shine)
shown (past tense of show)

stair (a step)
stare (to gaze)

stationary (not moving)
stationery (writing materials)

steal (to rob)
steel (alloyed metal)

straight (not bent or crooked)
strait (strict, rigid)

tale (a story)
tail (projection at the back of
       animals)

their (possessive of they)
there (adverb of place)

tier (a row)
tear (drop from eyes when crying)

vale (valley)
veil (cloth that covers)

vane (device to show wind direction)
vein (blood vessel)
vain (conceited; worthless)

waist (middle part)
waste (to squander)

ware (something to sell)
wear (to be dressed in; become less
       good by use)

weak (lacking strength)
week (seven days)

yoke (harness for oxen; part
       of a garment)
yolk (yellow of egg)

Lead and Led

The principal tenses of the verb to lead are lead, led, led.

Lead as a noun is a heavy metal.

XVIII. Fill in the blanks with lead or led.

1. The travelers were _____ to a little nook in the mountains.

2. Did the angels _____ the animals aboard the ark?

3. Who _____ them off the ark?

4. I am _____ to believe that _____ pencils were not used at the time of the flood.

5. Noah followed God's _____ for hundreds of years!

XIX. Use each homonym in a sentence that tells about the flood, rainbow, clouds, and color.

air	hole
heir	whole
allowed	lessen
aloud	lesson
ascent	pray
assent	prey
brake	rain
break	reign
coarse	right
course	write
complementary	rode
complimentary	road
dyeing	scene
dying	seen
fair	shone
fare	shown
forth	ware
fourth	wear

Confusing Words

Below are some confusing words that are often misspelled.

breath (noun, air taken into lungs)
breathe (verb, to exhale and inhale)

clothes (wearing apparel)
cloths (two or more pieces of cloth)

quiet (peaceful, not noisy)
quite (very)

advice (noun, counsel given)
advise (verb, to give counsel)

device (noun, something devised)
devise (a plan)

prophecy (noun, prediction of future)
prophesy (verb, to predict)

XX. Use at least seven words from the above list in good sentences. You may use more than one of the words in a single sentence.

Spelling Difficulties

Do you know how to spell the following words? Do you always spell them correctly in letters and reports? The hard parts are underlined.

XXI. The teacher can dictate the word list to you.

accept	knowledge
across	license
actually	linen
almost	loving
answered	minute
asked	off
biology	organized
break	prevent
busy	register
buy	sandwich
cabinet	senator
choose	similar
circular	social
courtesy	society
definite	speech
describe	stretch
description	stubborn
different	suburb
divide	sure
does	surprised
eager	syllable
easily	talent
elevator	thoroughly
enable	threw
exercise	through
fourth	toward
guardian	vinegar
guilty	visitor
initial	weather
interesting	woman
know	written

Look at the complete list of spelling words that can cause difficulties on page 58.

XXII. Write the story of the first rainbow using the words from the lists on pages 58.

Difficult Spelling Words

absence	column	guerrilla	omitted	siege
absorption	coming	guess	optimistic	skein
accommodate	commercial	handsome	origin	sophomore
ache	committee	hangar	original	specimen
acquaintance	confidence	harass	pageant	stationery
acquitted	control	height	parliament	statistics
across	controversy	heinous	perform	strictly
affidavit	convertible	history	permanent	succeed
again	counterfeit	hoarse	perseverance	sugar
aggravate	courteous	hour	picnicking	superintendent
aghast	curiosity	illiterate	pleasant	surgeon
all right	dealt	immediately	pneumonia	sympathize
ally	desperate	indictment	possessive	temperament
already	despise	indispensable	prairie	temporary
always	develop	innocent	prejudice	therefore
among	discipline	interfere	principal	tragedy
analysis	doctor	introduce	principle	typical
analyze	eighth	laboratory	professor	until
angel	eminent	legitimate	pursue	vacuum
angle	enough	leisure	quantity	vegetable
annual	envelope	library	quiet	vengeance
answer	everything	license	quite	warrant
appetite	exceed	literature	raise	wear
arctic	existence	magnificent	receipt	week
ascent	expedition	maneuver	receive	weird
awkward	expense	mathematics	referred	whether
bachelor	extraordinary	meant	reign	which
beggar	familiar	medal	repeat	whole
believe	fascinate	millionaire	repetition	women
benefit	fasten	miniature	rescind	won't
bicycle	February	minute	reservoir	would
boundary	forfeit	mortgage	restaurant	writer
bulletin	forty	muscle	rheumatism	writing
burglar	friend	mystery	rhyme	written
business	fulfill	necessary	ridiculous	wrote
cafeteria	genius	night	sacrifice	yacht
ceiling	government	ninth	schedule	
cemetery	governor	noticeable	secretary	
chauffeur	grammar	occasion	seize	
chocolate	gratified	occurrence	semester	
colonel	guarantee	often	separate	

The Brightening of the Rainbow

Never was a more beautiful thing than the rainbow. When does it come? Only after the old earth has been swept by a storm. Black, lonely, storm-swept day, but sundown brings enough to pay for it all. The clouds lift for a moment. From the lower edge gleams the sunshine. Wonder of wonders! Quickly God hangs out His bow of promise, and the heart leaps with joy and gladness.

But how is it done? What really gives us the rainbow? Listen! Out of the west shoots a pencil of light. No sign of a rainbow here; just one long, straight beam of light. But it strikes the raindrop, and like a flash it is torn into the glorious colors we love so well. Giving up self, separation, yielding is what did it. As long as the sunbeam held fast together, no violet, no purple, no red, nor green came to our view. Giving is the secret of the rainbow's brightness.

What makes the life beautiful? Learn the secret of the rainbow, and you will see. Giving, sacrifice, putting down all that is mean and selfish, conquering everything that would draw the soul into itself, and dwarf and make it narrow. You never saw a man or woman who was making the world a better place to live in that was not giving his or her life to be broken and used for others.

"But that means the altar," you say? Never say it! Never even think it! Say rather, "It means letting God have the life to do with as He sees best." It means pure, loving, joyful service. It means all the glory of the rainbow, instead of the one, lonely ray of sunlight. It means that God has touched the life and made it all glorious—glorious for time and for eternity.

It was a drop of rain that shattered the sunbeam. It may be a tear that will strike your life and bring out its real beauty. Will you say, "I can not have it so." Say rather, "I would have it so, Father, if it seemeth best to thee."

—*Edgar Vincent*

Spelling Lists,
Spelling Cards,
Testing,
and
Conclusion

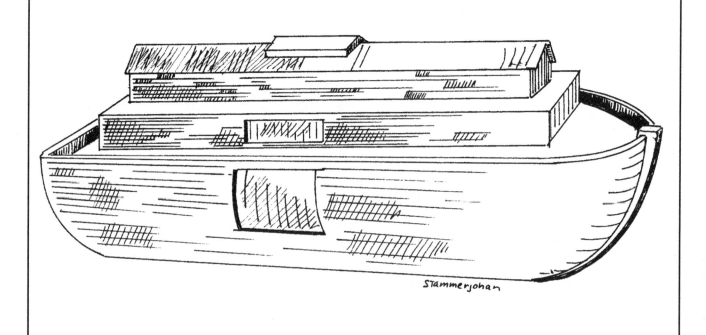

Making Spelling Lists From the Bible

"All scripture is given by inspiration of God, and is profitable for doctrine, for reproof, for correction, for instruction in righteousness: That the man of God may be perfect, throughly furnished unto all good works."
II Timothy 3:16, 17

1. Choose the verses the child is currently studying.

2. Have the child chart the individual words as shown in the sample on page 63. Do not repeat words already listed as you proceed through the verses. Be certain to have the child do the chart in pencil so words can be erased if placed in the wrong column. All erasing should be done carefully so as not to rub holes in the paper. Continue on the other side of the paper if necessary, as some columns will be longer than others. Use a new chart for each new list.

3. Follow the directions for doing "The Spelling Cards" on page 65.

4. Select words for the children to use in sentences that are thought up by themselves. Encourage them to make sentences concerning God, the Bible, nature, service to others, or practical things. Do not encourage sentences which focus on selfish thoughts and wants. Be sure they do not copy sentences directly from the Bible.

5. For spelling tests choose a number of words from each column according to each child's capability. Give time for study, going over the list with them word by word if necessary. Give the test, always aiming for total mastery. Study and test again any misspelled words. Stay with a given list until all words are mastered. Vary the testing by making it oral or letting the student make up a test and give it to the teacher.

The Psalms make wonderful spelling lists. Some excellent ones are: Psalm 27; 28; 29; 78; 81; 89; 90; 91; 92; and 93.

Genesis chapter's 1-8 can be used as a basic beginning for reading and spelling.

Exercise

XXIII. Choose a chapter from the Bible and make a spelling list from it.

Learn to spell all forms of the word.

Example

take
takes
taken
taketh
taking
took

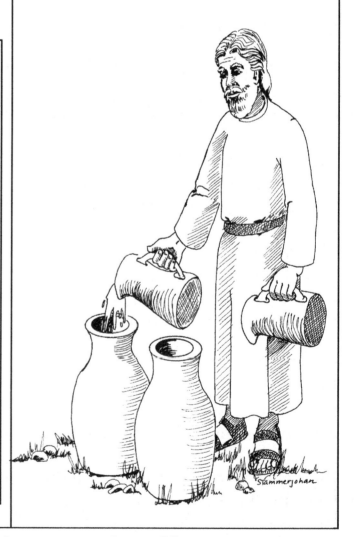

A Sample Word List

Spelling Lesson _____ Genesis 9:13-17 _____

One Letter	Two Letters	Three Letters	Four Letters	Five Letters	Six Letters	Seven or More
I	do	set	will	cloud	living	covenant
a	my	bow	come	shall	waters	between
	in	the	pass	token	become	remember
	it	and	when	earth		creature
	be	for	over	bring		destroy
	of	you	that	which		everlasting
	me	all	seen	every		established
	to	may	more	flesh		
	is	God	will	flood		
	no		look			
			upon			
			said			
			unto			
			Noah			
			this			
			have			

Spelling Word List

Spelling Lesson _____

One Letter	Two Letters	Three Letters	Four Letters	Five Letters	Six Letters	Seven or More

Spelling Card Instructions

1. Print the spelling word at the top of a 4" by 6" card.

2. Using a dictionary, write the word in syllables.

3. Put down how to pronounce the word.

4. Divide the rest of the card in half with a vertical line.

5.   a. Look up the word in *Strong's Exhaustive Concordance* and find an example of the spelling word used in its common or literal sense and write that verse on the left-hand side of your card. (Do not lose your place in *Strong's*.)

     b. Write the number of the word as it is used in the verse you selected from Strong's Concordance.

     c. Look up the *Strong's Concordance* definition and write it down after the number of the word. Use the italicized words of the definitions as these are the most accurate rendering of the translated definition.

     d. Go back to the dictionary and look for the definition that fits the verse you copied down from the Bible. Write that definition on the left side of the card. (You may also include other common definitions of the word if you like.)

6.   a. Use the right side of your card or turn it over, using a heading title of "Spiritual," "Symbolic," (or "Heavenly"). Look again through the concordance to see if you can find an example of the word used in a spiritual or symbolic sense. Not all words will have a spiritually symbolic sense.Write that sentence on the side or back side of your card.

     b. If you can tell the word's symbolic meaning from the text, write out a definition yourself as, most likely, the symbolic definition will not be found in Strong's or the dictionary. It is often something that is learned by comparing Scripture with Scripture. When you do find the symbolic meaning you will have a key that will help to unlock the mysteries of heaven's special code language.

7. Across the bottom of the front side of your index card write a complete sentence using your spelling word as it relates to the Bible lesson.

8. The etymology of the word, part of speech, synonyms, antonymns, and other forms of the word could be included.

9. What if the word cannot be found in *Strong's*? Use a synonym dictionary and find another word that has a similar definition. Follow the above proceedure but use the synonym word.

Place I – 1 card per week
Place II – 1-2 cards per week
Place III – 2-3 cards per week
Do spelling cards only every other week.

**(See example card
for a sample
on the next page.)**

Example of a Spelling Card

tongue
tongue (word in syllables)
_____ (how to pronounce the word)

Definitions

Common or literal: "...Every one that lappeth of the water with his tongue, as a dog lappeth, him shalt thou set by himself..." (Judges 7:5). 3956: instrument of licking, eating, or speech. **Literal definition:** the movable muscular structure attached to the floor of the mouth used in eating, tasting, and (in man) speaking. (You may include other common definitions here if desired, such as tongue = language.)	**Spiritual (symbolic):** "And suddenly there came a sound from heaven as of a rushing mighty wind, and it filled all the house where they were sitting. And there appeared unto them cloven tongues like as of fire, and it sat upon each of them. And they were all filled with the Holy Ghost, and began to speak with other tongues, as the Spirit gave them utterance" (Acts 2:2-4). **Spiritual (symbolic) definition:** tongues represent languages. Tongues is one of the gifts of the Holy Spirit enabling God's servants to communicate with those speaking a foreign language.

Use of the word relating to lesson: Jesus gave nature a tongue which speaks to our hearts of God's love.

The reason we are having the distinction between the literal definitions and the spiritual (symbolic) is to train the mind to see things spiritually as well as literally. This will be important when we study nature object lessons and Bible prophecy where God uses the literal to portray the spiritual. The child must be led to discern between the earthly things and spiritual things. Many times you will have to make up your own definitions for the symbolic meaning of the word. For example: A star is literally a heavenly body that shines in the night sky, but symbolically the Bible refers to the angels as stars and Jesus as a star. As you learn the symbolic meanings of things, you will be learning part of the language of heaven which is rich in wisdom. However, do not do so many cards that this becomes an endurance test for your child but rather make it an enjoyable exercise in learning about heavenly things.

Directions for Storage Box for the Spelling Cards

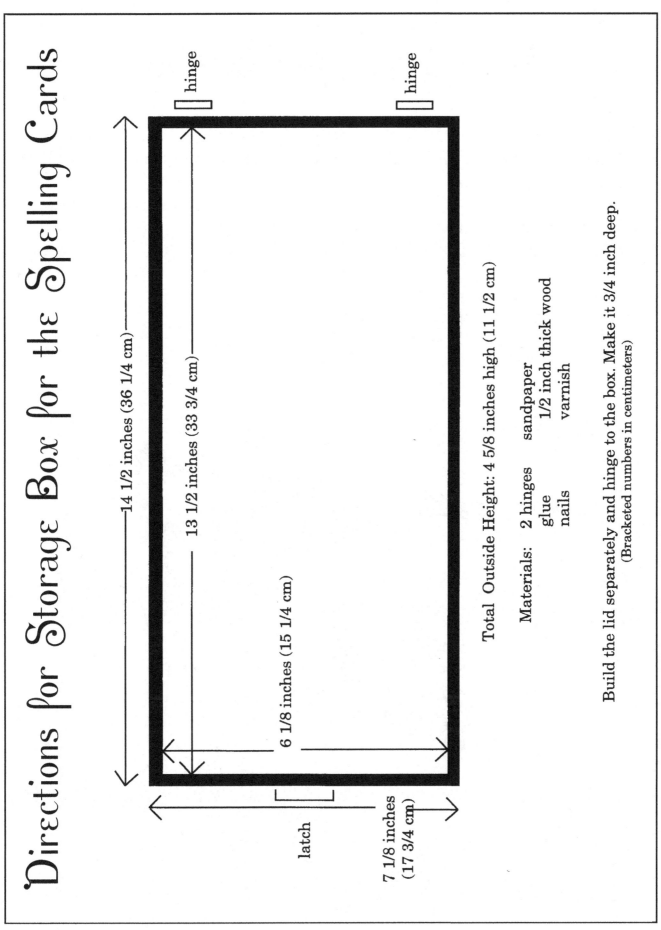

hinge

hinge

14 1/2 inches (36 1/4 cm)

13 1/2 inches (33 3/4 cm)

6 1/8 inches (15 1/4 cm)

latch

7 1/8 inches (17 3/4 cm)

Total Outside Height: 4 5/8 inches high (11 1/2 cm)

Materials: 2 hinges   sandpaper
             glue   1/2 inch thick wood
             nails   varnish

Build the lid separately and hinge to the box. Make it 3/4 inch deep.
(Bracketed numbers in centimeters)

Preparing for Testing

1. Make a spelling card.

2. Find a verse in the Bible using the word and memorize it.

3. Use the word in conversation and picture how to spell it.

4. Write each spelling word ten times when having difficulty spelling it.

5. Those who do poorly on their tests should write each word five times before the next test.

6. Have the student spell each word verbally or have a trial spelling test. Then he will know which words to concentrate on.

Methods of Testing

1. Dictate the words to write on paper or chalkboard.

2. Dictate words to be orally spelling. Have the student (a) say the word, (b) spell the word, (c) give a sentence using the word.

3. Dictate meaning and have student write the word. (Example: "think of again" – remember.)

4. Write words on the board or paper and omit letters to be filled in by the student. (Example: _establish_ed, es_tab_li_sh_ed, or e_stab_li_sh_ed.)

5. Match words and meanings with most common definition.

living — to come or grow to be
waters — alive
become — liquid that forms streams, lakes, and seas

6. Ask questions about the word. What does everlasting mean?

7. Give an antonym or synonym as a clue for the spelling word.

destroy – antonym = preserve
destroy – synonym = demolish

8. Give a prefix, root, and suffix to be constructed into a word.

ever
ing   = everlasting
last

9. Give the student letter cubes to arrange into correct words as you dictate the words.

10. Let the student give you a spelling test and then correct it without an answer key.

Conclusion

1. Laying a good foundation in reading, writing, and spelling is laying a good foundation for all of the academic subjects. We suggest you use *The Writing Road to Reading* program with your students.

The "Spelling Basics" section of this book makes a good review for the student who has had a good foundation laid. Review the spelling rules from *The Writing Road to Reading*.

Noah built his boat with the best materials and the finest of workmanship.

2. While laying a good foundation begin making word lists from Scripture.

While Noah built the ship he preached the word to those coming to observe this unusual sight.

3. The student will have regular spelling words from his academic subjects to make spelling cards. When more words are needed, use Bible verses to make word lists to supplement his assigned words.

Noah and his helpers cut great gopher (cypress) trees to build the vessel.

4. Test your student in the following ways:

- Dictate Bible verses.
- Write letters, stories, themes, or keep a journal.
- Give oral spelling tests.
- Give written spelling tests.

The test came for Noah and his family during the storm. The ship was secure, and their faith was strong.

5. The whole purpose of a good spelling program is to bring honor to Christ. In *"whatsoever ye do, do all to the glory of God"* (I Corinthians 10:31).

The covenant rainbow reminds us that Christ will never forget His children. It is a matter of honor, *"for them that honour me I will honour"* (I Samuel 2:30).

The Answer Key

Answer Key

Page 4

Lesson I
1. daughters of men

2. 120 years

3. giants

4. the children of the sons of God and the daughters of men

5. evil continually

Page 5

6. He repented that he had made man and it grieved him.

7. destroy man and beast, creeping things, and the fowls

8. Noah

9. just man, perfect in his generations

10. Shem, Ham, and Japheth

11. corrupt and filled with violence

12. all flesh

Page 5 continued

Lesson II
1. ark

2. gopher wood

3. length – 300 cubits (525 feet), breadth – 50 cubits (87.5 feet), height – 30 cubits (52.5 feet)

4. window and door

5. Noah and wife, sons and wives, two of every animal, food for man and animals

Page 6

6. He did all that God commanded him to do

7. *"Come thou and all thy house into the ark"*

8. because they were righteous

9. seven, two, seven

10. to keep seed alive upon the earth

11. 7 days

12. 600 years old

Answer Key

Page 7

Lesson III
1. after 7 days

2. fountains of the deep, windows of heaven

3. 40 days and 40 nights

4. they bare up the ark

5. 15 cubits

6. all flesh died upon the earth

7. Noah and all that were in the ark

8. 150 days

9. fire will burn it up

10. fire and brimstone from God

Page 8

Lesson IV
1. wind

2. See verses 1-3.

3. mountains of Ararat, seventh month

4. tenth month

Page 8 continued

5. raven

6. dove, found no rest

7. 601st year in the second month, 27th day

8. one year, 17 days

9. built an altar, offered sacrifices

10. not again curse the ground

11. seasons

Page 10

Lesson V
1. blessed Noah and his sons to be fruitful and multiply and replenish the earth

2. with fear

3. meat or flesh of animals

4. See Leviticus 17:10-11.

5. if a man killed a man he should be destroyed

6. an agreement

Answer Key

Page 10 continued

7. no universal flood again

8. rainbow, cloud

9. something given

10. Three: Shem, Ham, and Japheth

11. 350 years

Page 17

"I do set my bow in the cloud, and it shall be for a token of a covenant between me and the earth." Genesis 9:13

Pages 20-21

Teacher, check.

Page 34

I.
1. too, to

2. too, to

3. to, two, two

4. two

5. to, too

Page 36

II.
1. It's, its

2. It's, its

3. it's, its

4. its

5. It's its

III.
1. There, their

2. There

3. There, their

4. there, their

5. their, there

IV.
1. principle

2. principal

3. principal, principal

4. principle

5. principal

Answer Key

Page 37

V.
couldn't = could not (o)
didn't = did not (o)
doesn't = does not (o)
don't = do not (o)
hasn't = has not (o)
haven't = have not (o)
I'll = I will (wi)
I've = I have (ha)
mustn't = must not (o)
she's = she is (i)
shouldn't should not (o)
that's = that is (i)
there's = there is (i)
wasn't = was not (o)
we'll = we will (wi)
weren't = were not (o)
we've = we have (ha)
wouldn't = would not (o)
you'll = you will (wi)
you're = you are (a)

VI.
Teacher, check.

Page 38

VII.
Teacher, check.

VIII.
Teacher, check.

Page 39

IX.
1. loose, lose

2. loose

3. lose

4. loose, lose

5. lose, lose

6. lose

Page 40

X.
Teacher, check.

XI.
awfully
beautifully
cheerfully
continually
coolly
finally
formally
really
regretfully
usually

Answer Key

Page 42

XII.
Teacher, check.

Page 43

XIII.
Teacher, check.

Page 45

XIV.	
ancient	mischief
brief	neither
chief	reign
conceit	relieve
conscience	shield
deceit	shriek
fiend	sleigh
fierce	thief
freight	vein
friend	weigh
grief	weight
grieve	yield
height	

Page 46

XV.
1.

acquire 1	fortune 1
argue 2	leisure 1
associate 1	nonsense 5
broke rule 1	persistence 3
cause 5	please 5
dance 3	pleasure 1
deceive 2	responsible 4
desire 1	stole 1
ease 5	terrible 4
extreme 1	trouble 4
excuse 1	

2.

able 4	prepare 1
brave 1	sensible 4
courage 1	separate 1
gentle 4	serve 2
nice 1	true 2
organize 1	reverence 3
patience 3	voice 3
praise 5	wholesome 5
purpose 5	

3.

accommodate 1	outside 1
architecture 1	notice 3
escape 1	persevere 1
expense 5	possible 4
inside 1	serve 2
house 5	service 3
large 3	size 1

Answer Key

Page 46 continued

immense 5
invite 1
move 2

sure 1
vehicle 4

4.
awe 5
change 1
consequence 3
continue 2
disease 5
fatigue 2
freeze 5

grave 1
icicle 4
precipice 3
reprove 2
undesirable 4
waste 1

Page 47

5.
above 2
blue 2
circle 4
declare 1
exquisite 5
hope 1
life 1

love 2
orange 3
peace 3
picture 1
promise 5
shine 1
unchangeable 4

6.
circle 4
circumference 3
complete 1
entire 1
fierce 3
impossible 4
noise 5

reprove 2
science 3
strange 1
surface 1
unfortunate 5
voyage 1

Page 47 continued

7.
apple 4
article 4
cabbage 1
eagle 4
experience 3
evidence 3
goose 5
horse 5
moose 5
mouse 5

people 4
relative 2
shoe 5
sleeve 2
table 4
tissue 2
tortoise 5
treasure 1
vegetable 4

Page 49

1. duplicate
2. delicate
3. medicate
4. lubricate
5. locate
6. indicate
7. prognosticate
8. prevaricate
9. syndicate
10. abdicate
11. vindicate
12. confiscate
13. implicate
14. vacate
15. excommunicate
16. allocate
17. masticate

18. coruscate
19. fabricate
20. equivocate
21. obfuscate
22. dislocate
23. communicate
24. educate
25. dedicate
26. intricate
27. extricate
28. predicate
29. syllabicate
30. altercate
31. inculcate
32. desiccate
33. eradicate
34. intoxicate

Answer Key

Page 51

XVI.
nobody
everybody
somebody
anything
anywhere

Page 52

XVII.
Teacher, check.

Page 55

XVIII.
1. led

2. lead

3. led

4. led, lead

5. lead

Page 56

XIX.
Teacher, check.

XX.
Teacher, check.

Page 57

XXI.
Teacher, check.

XXII.
Teacher, check.

Page 62

XXIII.
Teacher, check.

I Need Thee, Precious Jesus

I need Thee, precious Jesus,
I hope to see Thee soon,
Encircled with the rainbow,
And seated on Thy throne.

There, with Thy blood-bought children,
My joy shall ever be
To sing Thy ceaseless praises,
To gaze, my Lord, on Thee!

—*F. Whitefield*

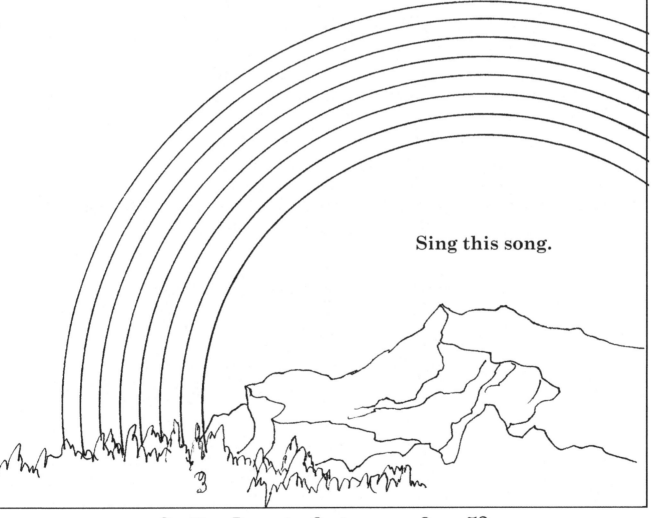

Sing this song.

The Wonderful World

**Even after the Flood the world is a beautiful place to live.
Memorize this poem.**

Great, wide, wonderful, beautiful world,
With the beautiful water above you curled,
And the wonderful grass upon your breast—
World, you are beautifully dressed!

The wonderful air is over me,
And the wonderful wind is shaking the tree;
It walks on the water and whirls the mills,
And talks to itself on the tops of the hills.

You friendly earth, how far do you go,
With wheat fields, that nod, and rivers that flow,
And cities and gardens, and oceans and isles,
And people upon you for thousands of miles.

Ah, you are so great and I am so small,
I hardly can think of you, world, at all;
And yet, when I said my prayers today,
"You are more than the earth, though you're such a dot;
You can love and think, and the world cannot."

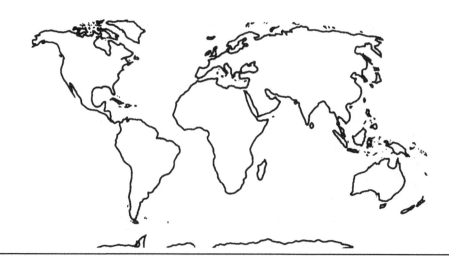

Outline of School Program

Age	Grade	Program
Birth through Age 7	Babies Kindergarten and Pre-school	*Family Bible Lessons* (This includes: Bible, Science–Nature, and Character)
Age 8	First Grade	*Family Bible Lessons* (This includes: Bible, Science–Nature, and Character) + Language Program (*Writing and Spelling Road to Reading and Thinking* [WSRRT])
Age 9-14 or 15	Second through Eighth Grade	*The Desire of all Nations* (This includes: Health, Mathematics, Music, Science–Nature, History/Geography/Prophecy, Language, and Voice–Speech) + Continue using WSRRT
Ages 15 or 16-19	Ninth through Twelfth Grade	9 – *Cross and Its Shadow I** + Appropriate Academic Books 10 – *Cross and Its Shadow II** + Appropriate Academic Books 11 – *Daniel the Prophet** + Appropriate Academic Books 12 – *The Seer of Patmos** (Revelation) + Appropriate Academic Books *or you could continue using *The Desire of Ages*
Ages 20-25	College	Apprenticeship

Made in the USA
Las Vegas, NV
26 September 2021